N

F

A

Not F*ing Around

The No Bullsh*t Guide for Getting Your Creative Dreams Off the Ground

This one goes out to the ones I love.

The courageous dreamers, makers, musicians, artists, writers, entrepreneures, filmmakers, storytellers. We are the ones who put our hearts on the line, our pedals to the metal.

We shine and crash and rise again. And again.

This book is dedicated to us.

Published by
Electron Unlimited LLC
8415 5th Avenue Northeast #305 • Seattle, WA 98115

Illustrations © Megan Hills • Layout and Design by Moses Gershbein

Second Edition

ISBN - Print: 978-0-692-89996-0 / eBook: 978-0-692-89998-4

For ordering information or special discounts for bulk purchases, educational
use or fund-raising, please contact Jeff Leisawitz at Jeff@JeffLeisawitz.com

Printed in the Unites States of America

CONTENTS

As far as I know, there are two ways of engaging with the world. At any given point you are either F*ing Around (**FA**) or Not F*ing Around (**NFA**).

F*ing Around is typical, obvious and what much of the world does much of the time. Clicking aimlessly online, shopping for sport, clocking into a gig that sucks your heart dry and denying the massive opportunities of this life is (in my book) F*ing Around.

There's a time and place for **FA**.

Without it we'd all go mad. But if it gets out of hand, it becomes a rut. And if you don't watch out, that rut sucks up your life.

Not Cool.

On the other hand,

Not F*ing Around is

the
PASSION
the
POWER
the
BANG! BANG! BANG!
that **Drives Us**
to
Take Real Action
to
Manifest a Life
Worth Living.

NFA is focus and freeform, karma and art, improv and strategy. When you're Not F*ing Around you know it. And so does everybody else in the room.

Nobody particularly likes to think about it, but our days on this Earth are numbered. You have limited time to do whatever you're gonna do. You could check out tomorrow or walk the planet for another fifty years, but sooner or later the jig is up. Game over.

This means at least one thing. Every moment, every breath, every thought, every action, every interaction, every intention and every everything else is precious.

Your life and your time on the planet is precious.

The meaning of life has been hotly debated since humans have had the capacity to hotly debate. At the end of the day, I have no idea what the Universe wants from us. For all I know, sitting around playing video games, drinking cheap beer, pounding pints of your favorite ice cream, and/or binge watching reality TV is a crucial aspect of the cosmic plan.

But I doubt it.

Humans are here to do stuff.

And the humans who find their truth and have the courage to act on it are the ones who change the world. Their worlds. And the worlds of those they touch.

It does take courage. There are ways to live that appear to be easier. But that's just an illusion.

The people who have the grit to act on their dreams are the ones who have sailed across forbidden seas, sketched out the math of the stars, built skyscrapers, bled heart stopping poetry, and done about a million other batsh*t crazy, sweet, delicious, fun and stunning other things.

Shortly before I graduated college (with a degree in Creative Writing with Perspectives from Philosophy, Religion and Psychology) my advisor sat me down and laid out some sobering truth.

"If you choose to be an artist, be prepared for 97% pain and rejection."

She followed up with another bit of harsh reality.

"Once you step off of this campus, the world is going to do everything possible to beat you down and stop you from learning, growing, creating and expanding."

At the time I didn't believe it. Twenty some years later I do.

I've seen so many people drop their passions and their purpose for no good reason. These are the dead-eyed masses who don't laugh from their bellies, don't have much to say, and avoid eye contact unless absolutely necessary. You know who I'm talking about.

But the dreamers are still out there.

The world marvels at their innovation. Their weirdness. Their talent. Their soulful swagger. These people are the ones who sparkle, giggle and grace us with their vision.

Whether it's hatching a plan for an erotic bakery, blowing off the day job to take pictures of monkeys in Asia, or learning how to brew up some kick ass beer in the garage, these are the ones you want to hang out with.

This is who you want to be.
This is who you could be.

Underneath all the crap, fear and social conditioning, this is who you were born to be. Your own special, freakish, imperfect, beautiful, f*ed up self is waiting to come out and play.

If you're reading this, you're ready.

This book is for you.

— **You're creative** even if you haven't really put out in years.

— **You burn (or smolder) with the punk rock spirit.** You question authority.

—You know that in your best moments **you tap into a universal creative force that's much bigger than yourself.** And you want to tap into it again on the regular.

No matter what project, path, tangent or vision you want to pursue, the ten steps in this book will point you in the right direction.

Stuck in a tailspin? Plotting some grand project and not doing a damn thing about it? Satisfied with mediocrity? Waiting for the right moment to make a move? Stifled by voices? Lost in the nonsense of it all?

You better keep reading. Yeah, I'm talking to you.

Stick with me and you're bound to acquire some wisdom, find some motivation, and/or make something happen. At the very least, you'll confront your **Ic*** and demand some satisfaction.

The challenge here is simple— to rev up, keep it on the road, and step on the gas. If you hang around and put some time and energy into the process, I can pretty much guarantee you'll make some progress.

*Read on. Learn to battle The Ic. (And kick its ass.)

In these pages I'll do my best to help you start, focus, follow through and complete your goals. I'll squeeze everything I've got out of my little brain cell, my battered heart and my years of experience to help you push forward on your personal missions and projects.

So what makes me so qualified to spout about this stuff?

Maybe because I've been living it since the night I picked up my first electric guitar and worked out the opening riff to one of my favorite Bowie songs. Or maybe it was the day my grandfather took me into his darkroom and we watched images magically appear on wet paper through a mind blowing chemical reaction. Or perhaps it was the Saturday afternoon I saw *Star Wars* with my dad and believed that I could use the Force too.

> **Maybe I'm qualified because I've battled armies of demons, years of depression, enemies both internal and external, and a mountain range of obstacles.**

Let's not forget the professional cheaters and liars in the music biz. The dysfunctional legions of Hollywood types. The street level hustlers and flakes. The corporate entities that claim to be 'artist friendly' while selling your blood for fractions of pennies on the dollar. The apathetic masses. Or myself.

Maybe I'm qualified because I practiced NLP (NeuroLinguistic Re-Patterning), helping clients untangle their subconscious blocks to get the party started. Or trained as a Life Coach. Or clocked in as a college instructor to teach songwriting to young rockers.

Whatever makes me qualified, I've somehow managed to shoot about a million photos, win an international award for my music, release a bunch of albums, get my tunes onto tons of tv shows, and make an internationally distributed short film. Plus, I've dug into a pile of other crazycool side projects along the way.

I've made art with nude models and octopus tentacles (although not at the same time). Turned a barista into a superhero. Tie-dyed hundreds of t-shirts at Camp Log-n-Twig. Penned sci-fi screenplays. And somehow managed to pay the rent.

And yes, I've bashed my head against about a thousand walls along the way. There has been blood.

This book is all about sharing what I've learned so that you can bash your head against fewer walls.

ARE YOU READY TO NFA?

LET'S ROCK!

DISCOVER
What
You
Love (AND WHY)

You may already know what you love. F*ing fantastic! Your love may be focused on one pursuit, one idea, one thing. Or it might be a ton of stuff. Good for you. Very cool. Keep your pants on for a minute while I dig into it with those who are still stumped.

Not sure you know what you love or what you want to do?

Face the facts. You're not looking hard enough.

This world is amazing in infinite ways and there is more opportunity now than ever before to discover, explore and make cool things.

Seriously. Remember when you were a kid and you were blown away by pretty much everything? Fire trucks. Lipstick. Multi-colored popsicles.

As a child your sense of wonder and imagination is free. The world hasn't stomped on your fascination with everything yet.

You were never bored because everything was new, a mystery. And some of those mysteries were captivating.

How do I build a dam in the creek down the street without coming home covered in mud?

What are the stars made of?

Why aren't there pickle flavored cookies?

You may notice something about imagination, fascination, wonder and mystery. They always include questions. Why? Because **questions take us deeper.** They turn us on to layers of exploration and understanding. Our brains are built to question the Universe.

Maybe you can construct a dam without getting busted (again) by your mom.

Maybe someone already figured out what the stars are made out of. And maybe someday you can figure out something new about those twinkly little lights in the sky.

Maybe if you tweaked the recipe, pickle flavored cookies could be a big hit this Thanksgiving.

If you don't know what you love, start asking questions. Ask the best questions you can squeeze out of your skull. The best questions you can dream.

Question everything. Soon you'll find your passion.

Surf the net in directions you don't normally turn. Go to the library or bookstore and browse shelves that you haven't seen. Talk to every stranger you can find and ask them what they love. Or just call your mom. She'll be happy to remind you about the oddball **NFA** obsessions you had when you were a kid.

The more you look, and the more questions you ask, the sooner you'll find your thing. And please, get weird about it. Anything goes.

Once you know what you love, it's easy to figure out what to do with it. Learn more? Teach others? Make something out of it? Do something with it? Play with it?

Whatever lights your fire is the right answer. But it's just one possible answer. There are many.

Okay. Now that everybody knows what they love, and what they want to do with it, there's one more question to ask.

The question is why? *Why* do you love it? This question is bigger than it seems. *Why* drills down to the core of your passion.

I love figure skating because *I'm astonished by the beauty of grace and movement.*

I love building sculptures out of steel because *this world is fleeting and I want to create something permanent on this Earth before I check out.*

I love teaching people how to bake pies because *it reminds me that there is sweetness in the world and I want to share it in pie form.*

The *why* is the *intention*. To learn something. To explore something. To make something. To master a practice.

Intention is BIG.

If your intention is external, no matter what you do, your efforts will not be fueled with love and won't pay off in the vast and beautiful ways that matter.

External intentions (or motivations) include:

- Your girlfriend might think you're cool if you do it.

- You might make a fortune even though you couldn't care less about what you're doing.

- Your fifth grade teacher said you couldn't do it (so you're going to prove her wrong even though she forgot your name decades ago).

- Your buddy won't stop nagging you about it so you might as well give it a shot.

Internal intentions (or motivations) include:

- You're so f*ing psyched to work on your thing that you can barely sleep.

- You want to understand how it works. Just because.

- You know you can do it better, faster, stronger, more efficiently. You want to prove it to yourself and the world.

- You simply need to share your passion, express yourself, and/ or teach something to someone who cares about the same things you do.

Like pretty much everybody, I used to be driven by the external. After dropping out of school and starting my own tie-dye business, I eventually moved across the country to southern California to push forward with my college degree. It was finally time to pick a major but I was baffled.

I was getting pressure from the folks, the real world was right around the corner, and I was scared. Sh*tless.

- **Sleepless nights.**
- **Cold sweats.**
- **Panic attacks.**

Thank Goddess I had enough sense to follow my authentic self.

When you know what you love and why you love it, you're almost good to go. But without a plan or even a specific goal, it's time to check in. For me, it took a midnight ride through the orange groves to clue in.

Much to the chagrin of my parents, I (eventually) graduated with the aforementioned dubious degree—*Creative Writing with Perspectives from Philosophy, Religion and Psychology*—and never looked back. Although in retrospect it would've been a wise move to take some web design classes.

Believe it or not, your conscious mind doesn't know everything. In fact, it's really good at some stuff, really lousy at other stuff. When your conscious mind drops into your monkey mind—chattering away in circles and not really going anywhere—the truth gets obscured.

That's why you need to find a quiet place. A quiet room. A quiet walk. A quiet mind.

Breathe. Feel. Don't think.

Pull the thing you love into your heart.

If you don't sizzle inside, keep looking around and exploring the world. Keep asking questions.

But if your heart lights up, turns on, beats faster and expands in your chest, you're gold.

On one of those sleepless nights back in college I rode my mountain bike through the orange groves on the outskirts of town. The moon beamed down. The scent of warm citrus wafted through the air. I stopped. Sat under a tree. Breathed in real deep.

In that moment I knew who I was. I knew at least the general direction I needed to go.

I sped through the night back to my dorm room and slept soundly for the first time in months.

Declare
Your
Dream

Flash back with me to college (again). I went to a hippie school (surprise!) where I was fortunate enough to design my own major. But there was a catch. I had to write an essay about why I wanted to do my thing and what I wanted to do. Then I had to defend it in front of the registrar, my advisor, a bunch of professors and peers.

Eek.

There's a reason why football games are played in front of raging crowds. There's a reason why lovers say 'I do' while their friends and family smile and gaze upon them (and wonder what's for dinner). There's a reason why tens of thousands of people cram onto the Mall in DC in the freezing cold to watch the new president take the oath.

Declaring your intention in front of others makes it real.

It keeps us accountable. Everybody knows that when all is said and done, there's generally much more said than done. Sports teams, lovers and presidents know they better walk the walk. Especially after they say it in public.

It's easy to tell yourself (in the privacy of your own head) that you're going to get that website online by the end of the month. It's a piece of cake to whisper through the neurons of your gray matter that you're going to spend six hours this weekend writing that play about geriatric superheroes. It's a simple matter of self deception to swear up and down that this is the year you make a forty foot bamboo robot and drag it to Burning Man.

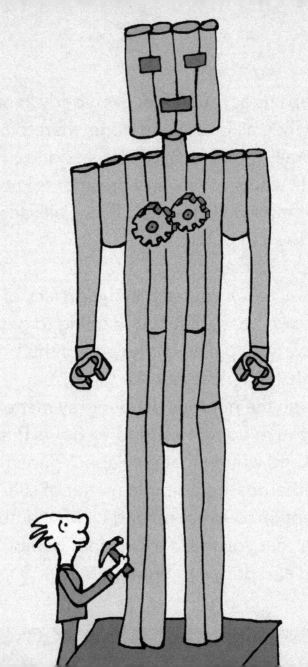

But as we all know, any half-assed rationalization can drop your dreams down the priority list as soon as a shinier cookie, shorter robot, or easier option comes around the corner.

Don't feel bad. One could argue that self-deception is human nature. Why do something difficult (even if it's a huge turn on) if it's not necessary?

If you're sitting around your place and you're starving, you gotta eat something. Some folks are gonna spend an hour making zucchini pasta and almond butter basil pesto. Others will heat up a hot dog in the microwave.

Both ways get the job done. One is much, much easier than the other. But for someone who likes to cook (and/ or likes to eat), the former option is the much better choice. Even though it takes more effort.

Did you catch that?

Sometimes the better choice takes much more effort.

This is really key, so pay attention.

Laying around watching *Simpsons* reruns is great. Believe me, I've done it. But if you always choose Homer and the gang over taking action, nothing gets done. And you want things to get done. So, just like our sports guys, lovers and presidents, it's generally a good idea to declare your dream to your people.

Of course, your first people are your family.

As a kid, the words of your parents can launch you into the stratosphere or crash you into a brick wall before lift off. Many, many, many young dreams have been thwarted by well-meaning parents who want their kids to be safe, secure and get a decent job at some point. Fair enough. But here's the rub. People only know what they know.

They assume what's good for them is good for everyone, especially their children. This is simply not always true.

At any age, it's a bold step to announce your creative intentions to your folks with respect and resolve. But you don't really need to do it to their faces. Saying it out loud in an empty room, or writing a letter (and not sending it) jets a powerful message out into the Universe that you're ready to break away from old patterns and expectations that don't serve you. This is bigtime **NFA**.

If the words on this page make you uncomfortable, you really need to take this advice.

After you write your letter or deliver your monologue to an empty room, it's time to step it up. Make it real.

You could declare your dream online, although I wouldn't recommend it. Why? Because social media is a constant stream of largely disposable information and your friends won't remember your heartfelt declaration twenty minutes after it happens.

Pick your circle carefully. Invite your gang to get together and then tell them what's up. Tell them the plan. Not just a vague statement like, "I'm going to get my sh*t together and build that exotic frog terrarium." **Instead, make sure your declaration includes these four things:**

1. **What exactly you're going to do.**

2. **Why you're going to do it.**

3. **When you'll do it and when it'll be done.**

4. **How your circle will know it happened.**

What matters most here is that you are held accountable.

You need feedback, a cheerleader and at least one witness who will hold your feet to the fire.

Shouting it out to your people is great. And you probably should do it. But for many, this is treading in dangerous waters. Your pals may be negative, mired in their own nonsense, or just lost in a fog. You may not get the happy response that you deserve. Just be ready.

If the word is flat or the whole thing turns into an energy suck, it's cool. It happens. Sparking up and shining bright will hit your gang on one level or another. Your enthusiasm and resolve will be heard and felt. Perhaps they will soon alter their own **NFA** ratio.

If your peeps don't cut it, find some new ones. With a little help from the internet you can easily connect with zillions of peers who are actually into what you're into. Start with Meetup.com and take it from there. You kinda wanted some new pals who were into your thing anyway.

While it's great to have people around to support your vision, there's someone more important that needs to get on board. Without their full support and commitment it just ain't gonna happen. I'm talking about you.

Find a quiet time and space to write down everything you told your gang. Except now you can craft it, expand it, declare it.

When it's all perfect, sign it. Snap a pic. Email it to your people. Pin it on the wall.

Make. It. REAL.

Time
Travel

WITH
Your
Future
Self

We run around all day long watching the clock, avoiding getting run over by buses, getting home in time for dinner. There is definitely something to say for time and space. But it's overrated.

Somewhere along the line you may have felt an inkling, a feeling or an intuitive whisper that time and space are not really as solid as they appear. Trippy, but true.

Since the beginning, mystics have claimed that time is an illusion. These days quantum physicists are filling in the details. You occasionally know what's up in those transcendent moments of music, sex, nature or whatever else gets you there.

I'm certainly not going to claim to know the secrets of time and space, but I will claim this—

From the present moment we can influence the future.

Obviously. But it's more subtle (and more powerful) than you might suspect. And it works in ways that look like magic.

Study after study shows that people who visualize an outcome for themselves—shooting a perfect free throw, making a million dollars, figuring out a solution to a complex creative problem—are many times more likely to actually do it than those who don't.

This is an **NFA** basic psychological/ spiritual technology. It might not seem like much. But it works.

I wrote a song a few years ago in which I somehow managed to compose a super funky bassline that I could hear in my head, but couldn't actually play properly. I practiced that sucker again and again and again. My fingers ached. I was getting frustrated, but I didn't want to wuss out and write something easier.

Instead, I sat there in the dark and conjured up Geddy Lee, the otherworldly bassist from the rock band Rush. I watched him play my bassline with absolute perfection. I could hear the nuance, the power and the precision. Then I picked up my guitar. I nailed the song in the next take.

Do this now

Get yourself into your quiet room and comfy chair. Imagine someone who has the qualities or the outcome that you want to acquire. A person who is clearly **NFA**. See them in your mind. If you want to be an amazing dancer, imagine your amazing dancer friend, or some other famous dancer, doing their thing.

Watch them closely. Then step inside of them.

As you move into their minds and bodies, feel what it's like to be them.

Feel the way they move. Feel what they eat. How they sleep. Discover their habits. Feel the grace and fluidity of their movements. Become the essence of who they are and what they do.

Got that? Kinda intense, right?

Now create a picture of yourself in your mind right next to the one you just created. In this image, see yourself doing the same things, feeling the same feelings, knowing the same stuff . Now step into that picture. Breathe into that picture. Notice what it feels like to have the skills and practice and energy and grace of an amazing dancer. Because now that dancer is you.

This is
Your Future Self
Waiting to Happen.

Energize this moment.

Feel it deeply. Breathe it in.

This is very important. You must feel the experience.

The more deeply you feel it, the more powerful it becomes.

Get into the heart of the feeling and let it wash over you. Thank your future self. Ask your future self what you need to do to meet him or her in the future. Pay attention.

This is deep, valuable, subconscious information that will help you get to wherever you want to go.

When you're ready, come back to the present. (You probably shouldn't drive a car or run heavy machinery for awhile.)

Congratulations! That was a serious **NFA** move. You just time traveled to a potential future, seeded it with the possibility of your desire, and created a powerful pathway to manifest it.

YOU
JUST ROCKED
THE TIME/SPACE
CONTINUUM.
YOU
AND YOUR
FUTURE SELF ARE
SUPERSTARS!

Start
Before
You're
Ready

You're never really ready. Neither am I. And neither is anybody else. So you might as well step up to it right about now. Do you think a new president is ready to run the country? No f*ing way.

You will never feel fully prepared to do whatever it is that you want to do.

You won't even feel totally capable after you've been doing your thing for years. Self doubt is etched into our psyches. It's there to help keep us alive and make us think twice before taking stupid risks. But you gotta be a chump to let it stop you from doing your thing.

I had a friend who was a teacher at a local college. He did one-on-one lessons with music students in songwriting and home recording. I was (and still am) a songwriter/ producer with hundreds of songs under my belt. I thought this job was just about the coolest thing ever. One day he quit and passed the gig to me. Three weeks later, I was gearing up to teach my first lesson.

Very cool. Except I had never taught anybody anything before. I knew what I was talking about, songwriting-wise, but these kids were music majors. I couldn't read music and I didn't have half a clue about composition and theory. Although I had a proven history and plenty of success in the music biz, I was intimidated by these kids. Even the freshmen.

When the semester kicked in, I faltered, freaked out, got a clue, learned a few things about college students, begged my boss for advice, and somehow plowed forward to the end of the semester. It was full-on crazy town.

But check this out... I ended up with something like 96% positive student evaluations.

When I started I was absolutely sure I sucked as a teacher. Absolutely. Sure.

But apparently these students learned something. By jumping into the deep end I got it together as fast as I could.

We only get experience by doing things.

You aren't a rocket car inventor until you invent a rocket car.

You aren't a cat juggler until you juggle some cats.

You aren't a sushi chef until you spin up some caterpillar rolls.

Invent. Juggle. Spin. Start before you're ready. It's the NFA way.

The title to this chapter is complete crap. Sorry. Please let me explain.

How do we learn? By doing something wrong until we get it right. It happens when you attempt to walk for the first time. When you touch the hot stove. When you try to memorize your multiplication tables.

The first time is nearly always a disaster. But sooner or later you stand on your own two feet, keep your hands off the burner and dazzle your calculus teacher (and your mom) with your rock star math skills.

The key here is 'sooner or later.'

Wanna be a great photographer? Get a f*ing camera and start taking pictures. Wanna direct a play? Find some actors and a stage. Wanna tear it up in the kitchen? Score some exotic ingredients and turn up the heat.

Will you fail on some level the first time you try? Probably. You may screw it up the tenth time too. Good!

You're doing it right (by doing it wrong).

Do you think the first song the Beatles wrote was a hit? Nope. They played countless covers and penned tons of tunes before they landed on the charts. Think Einstein came up with the theory of relativity on some random Saturday night after a few beers? Maybe. But he cranked his brain down a thousand dead ends before it all came together.

These guys failed fast. They knew the trick.

The faster you fail, the faster you learn, the faster you succeed.

But the pithy title of this chapter is actually horsesh*t. Why? Because if you look at the world in a positive and productive way, there is no failure, only feedback. Catch that? Even a full-on, five star cluster-hump has some redeeming quality, something to learn.

Many millionaire entrepreneurs go bankrupt several times before they hit it big. They crash fast and they crash hard. They learn from their mistakes. Then they make the millions.

Fail fast in whatever you do. It's the **NFA** way. Just remember it's not actually failure. It's quick steps towards success.

Squeeze all the wisdom out of your mistakes. Ask questions from every direction. Dig deep into your intention, process and outcome. The keys to future successes are hiding somewhere in the shadows.

A few years ago I took a class. Improv Comedy. Soooo scary. Why? Because you never knew what was gonna happen every time you stepped out in front of the class.

I won't give you the whole rundown of the improv philosophy, but one of the tenets struck me as particularly wise. It works for improv and it works for life too, since life is the biggest improv stage you're ever gonna step on.

The philosophy is simple:

**Say
"Yes, and_____."**

That's it. A big step in successfully
improvising with another human being
(and the world in general) is to say
yes—to agree with whatever is in front
of you. Then add something of value.

You get the point.

This works great on stage and in class. But it works even better in real life.

You just need to accept the reality of whatever the situation is—whether you like it or not—then add something of value to it.

Imagine your zillionaire Italian grandmother just passed away. Instead of inheriting her vast fortune, you end up with a top-notch 1950's espresso machine. Say Yes! to some schmancy homemade designer coffee drinks.

Your mom wants you to take eight gallons of different colors of paint to the household hazardous waste disposal site. Yes! Except you get diverted to your place where you do the 'modern abstract painting' that you always dreamed of in your guest bathroom. Win. Win.

Life offers countless opportunities. Saying Yes! to every single one of them would be a bit much. You probably don't want to try meth with the drug dealer on the corner, give all of your dough to the sketchy guy in the cheap suit with the 'guaranteed' investment opportunity, or test drive a mad scientist's anti-gravity vehicle (during rush hour).

But there are plenty of amazing opportunities where Yes! is the correct answer.

Say it. Write it.
Paint it on the walls.

Be the Shining Star You Are

Why are movies, TV shows, novels and stories such a big deal? Because they're dramatized, idealized crystallizations of the best (and worst) of human experience.

In nearly every great story a hero is faced with a big choice. This choice, if accepted, pushes the hero into a new world where he must overcome increasingly difficult obstacles until he finally makes it across the finish line. Then his life changes.

Outwardly, he has achieved his goal. On the inside he has fundamentally evolved as a person. He has grown, learned something, gotten bigger, kinder, saved the world, whatever.

This is commonly known in literary circles as the hero's journey.

When it's well done, it's absolutely captivating. It's captivating because each of us is on our own version of the hero's journey.

We are all heroes.

When Luke Skywalker leaves his home planet he steps into a world that's much bigger than anything he had experienced before. When he turns off the targeting scope and fires one shot into the Death Star he acknowledges his faith in the Force, beyond any scientific reason or good common sense. His faith pays off. Luke is officially a superstar after saving a defenseless planet. Nice work, buddy. **NFA** for sure.

You and I are not likely to save any planets any time soon, but we are constantly faced with opportunities to step up our game.

Perhaps you could fix the piece-of-crap photocopier again, even though you didn't break it (and you're almost certainly going to get toner all over your new shirt).

Perhaps you could buy coffee for your co-worker (again) even though he isn't likely to return the favor before the next solar eclipse.

Maybe it's finally time to step up and sing karaoke to "Don't Stop Believin'" with the same zest, verve and gusto that you do in the shower or when you race down the freeway.

One of the reasons that people love the protagonists in their favorite movies is because these characters have the guts to do things that we mortals are afraid of doing ourselves.

How many times have you seen an attractive or interesting person across the room and not moved an inch? Have you ever had some choice words to say to your clueless boss that never managed to escape your lips?

Remember how you felt when the guy in the dumb romantic comedy walked right up to the hottie and delivered an amazing pick-up line? Or when the demure office worker told her so-called superior that he didn't know squat about squat?

We love these moments because we're generally too chickensh*t to do these things ourselves.

It's a powerful **NFA** move to consider yourself the writer, director and actor in the movie of your life.

Every minute is a chance to write, act and live in a better story.

The story can be anything you want it to be. It can have more action, more excitement, more creativity, more love, more money. It can also have less stress, less bullsh*t, less hassle, less nonsense.

As you may have guessed, I had a rough start in 'higher education.' Within a year or two of escaping high school I got hit hard with some serious stuff— a friend died, another committed suicide, another had serious health issues. Yet another was sexually assaulted. It was not a good time in my world. The pain around me was relentless. I was alienated, depressed, confused and scared.

After transferring schools several times and dropping out (to start the tie-dye business), I got accepted to an amazing college in California. Weeks before I was about to ship out and move across the country, I found myself with some very cold feet.

Until this point, I didn't have it in me to make it through college. I had always come running back to my parents and the safety of my hometown, even though it was very obviously time for me to move on. I was freaking out and seriously considered bailing on the move. A voice in my head kept yapping at me. "Sink or swim. Sink or swim."

I had a tremendous choice to make. Fortunately, I sucked it up, got on that plane, and moved to California.

I had a very successful few years at that school. I stayed on the west coast and slowly built a really cool life here. But sometimes I wonder what would have happened if I had chosen differently. I might still be stuck in my parents' basement. I might be working a job that doesn't turn me on. I might have let fear rule my world, my relationships and my work.

Be your own protagonist.
Be the shining star you are.

Buy your f*ing ticket to California.

Play It Un-Safe

As you may have noticed, humans are delicate creatures with oversized brains that tend to get themselves into trouble. I could write a book about all the flavors and ways we screw ourselves up between the ears, but here's one specific way that you really should watch out for.

Everybody wants freedom. Everybody wants security. It's tough to have both at the same time.

This may mean different things to different people, but it boils down to one thing. Stick with what you've got (or what appears to be a good bet) or step out into the world for more adventure, more love, more fulfillment. Something better.

This might mean investing a chunk of your savings into your dream business even though you were gonna use the dough to go to Maui. It might mean auditioning for the community theater production of Grease (since you've known all the words to the song "You're the One that I Want" by heart since junior high). It might mean asking your boss for a shot at a project that you're only semi-qualified for. It might be a million things.

So here's the deal. People tend to play it safe, especially as they get older. And yes, that can be a good thing. But it can also kill (or stunt, or damage, or destroy) your heart, spirit and power.

Even the most complex choices generally come down to two opposing, motivating forces— fear and love.

Fear keeps us stuck. It keeps us small. It keeps us feeling as if we're safe. But we're not really safe, especially from change. Things will change whether we want them to or not. Tough luck.

Decisions and actions (or inactions) based on fear have value. We need to be safe (or feel safe) in many ways. But if too many decisions are based on fear, your world becomes stagnant, predictable and boring. It won't transform, flow or bend.

Your life is always the result of your choices.

If fear drives your choices, fear will overtly (or subconsciously) rule your life. And that sucks.

Decisions based on love are very different. These choices may feel uncertain. They may appear foolish to yourself and others. They may put your money, your time or your heart at risk.

You gotta be willing to face some risk if you want a shot at a real reward.

Okay. Now I'm gonna get metaphysical and weirder. Buckle up.

The Universe is a reflexive energy system.

What you put into it is what you get out of it. Call it karma, call it whatever you like. Whatever you think, however you act, and whatever you believe, projects into the Universe in mysterious ways and sooner or later comes back to you.

The Universe is always quietly attempting to pull events and people together to serve everyone's highest good.

It is conspiring blessings upon all of us all of the time. Even if you don't believe it, it's still true. If you do believe it, the cosmos amplifies the karma, blessings, goodness and coincidences to make cool sh*t happen for you and everyone around you.

This goodness is always there, but we need to be on the lookout for it. Sometimes it's in disguise. When we acknowledge the good and make decisions based on real, genuine love, the Universe kicks back in our favor.

The Universe is Love and wants the best for every living thing.

What's my point?

There is more safety in actions that are inspired by choices based on Love than on choices based on Fear.

Sometimes this might appear to be playing it unsafe. And sometimes your intended outcome is not going to look anything like what you're actually gonna get. But if your heart is open wide and tapped into your truth, everything will fall into place sooner or later. You will be safe. In fact, you'll resolve the need for both safety and freedom by letting go.

Let go. Play it unsafe. Choose Love.

The Universe will guide you towards your highest good.

It's easy to blame others for our failures, insecurities and pretty much everything else.

A common strategy is to start with your parents and all the ways they failed you. If you manage to work through that, a great target is always the system, society or The Man. If you get bored with that, just point your angst towards your neighbor, your boyfriend or whoever is in your way at the moment.

Sure, these people may have hurt you or thwarted your progress in some ways, but it's time to move on. To heal. To take responsibility. Their days of wrecking your efforts are over. Let it go.

Here's the truth. The one who puts the most time and effort into sabotaging our lives is ourselves.

We are often our own worst enemy. Of course this can come in many forms, but I want to call out one aspect that does particular damage to our creativity, motivation and joyous exploration of the world. That would be our **Inner Critic**.

I prefer to call that little snotball **The Ic**. (Pronounced: Ick)

The Ic has killed so many dreams, crushed so many souls, mangled so many projects, procrastinated and frozen so many great ideas, that it is truly the unseen supervillain of the creative spirit.

If the Ic gets the right word in at the wrong moment your whole vision will be flushed before the party even gets started.

The Ic is that voice that tells you that you're not good enough, smart enough, creative enough, experienced enough, clever enough, bold enough, daring enough, (etc., etc.) to do what your heart knows you want and knows you can do.

If you listen to the Ic you will sooner or later make decisions based on fear. And we all know what happens then.

But here's the funny thing. The Ic doesn't actually have its own voice. The Ic just rips off everybody else's lines.

The Ic is great at channeling your grade school art teacher, the one who said you were an idiot for painting flying saucers with monkey pilots.

The Ic may take the form of your well-meaning parents who screamed at you in high school to kill your dreams in favor of pursuing a real job.

The Ic loves to copy the tone of your ex-girlfriend who would smugly nod when you got excited about something.

She thought you were a moron even if she didn't actually say it. She may not have actually spoken but the Ic is happy to lend a voice to that soul numbing response.

Here's the bad news. The Ic is built into everybody. It ain't never gonna disappear forever. But that's okay, because the Ic serves a valuable purpose (I'll monologue on that in a minute).

Here's the good news.

> # The Ic is not running the show, even though it'll do anything it can to make you believe it is.

There are lots of ways to shut the Ic up, to get **NFA** on its ass. The first and biggest way is simply to let it know that it is powerless. To let it know that it's not on the payroll. Not the boss.

Do this now

Close your eyes and invite the Ic into a room in your mind. The Ic appears. It knows it doesn't need an invite (because it crashes the party constantly) but it's happy to show up on demand. The Ic loves airtime.

Let the Ic yak and rant and moan. If it's on its game, right about now it'll be riffing about how stupid this exercise is and what a chump you are for buying this book in the first place.

Let it do its thing.

The Ic's days are numbered.

Now imagine a big knob, like on a stereo. Grab the knob in your mind (and/ or out in the air) and slowly turn it counterclockwise. Listen closely. The Ic's voice gets quieter as you turn the knob. Cool.

Turn it up for a sec. The Ic starts yelling. Soon it'll be out of breath so you might as well let the Ic shout it out. After all, it's just doing its job.

When ready, turn the Ic's volume the whole way down. The Ic is out of commission.

If you really wanna f* with the Ic, check out some of those other dials and controls next to the big knob. Play around with them. They make the Ic's voice sound like a chipmunk. Or stutter. Or get sleepy and nod off. Really, you can use these controls to f* with the Ic as much as you like. The point is to let it know that you're chief. Whenever the Ic makes an unwanted appearance out there in the real world, just pull up the knob in your mind and shut it off. Easy.

Seriously, this works. It may take some practice but it works. Try it.

Okay, I mentioned earlier that the Ic does have some beneficial functions. This stuff is a bit advanced. It's like the Force. You better know what you're doing or you're gonna get sucked into the dark side. But if properly harnessed, the Ic can be a driver towards excellence.

All great artists, business types, athletes, and humans in general, allow the Ic to speak, to a point. It helps push them past mediocrity. It helps push them past 'really good,' and even beyond 'great.'

The Ic can help fuel the focus and energy it takes to achieve true excellence.

But beware. The Ic is one slippery bitch. Dialogue with the Ic is dangerous. For now, I recommend shutting it up and kicking some ass without listening to the yammer.

When you're ready, and you've got the Ic right where you want it, it might be worthwhile to chat up a quick conversation once in awhile. Listen to what it says. It may have a good point now and then. But then say goodbye and turn up the **NFA**. Time to get back to business.

Crush
ON THE
Process

It's all about the process.

A poet I once knew (who also moonlighted as an undercover guru) told me this many years ago. She said that a poet is not someone with a stack of poems on her desk. A poet is not someone with published works or a teaching gig. A poet is someone who writes poetry. As in, they actually do it. They write poems.

This is huge.

Although there is certainly value in sharing the poems, the real value (for the writer) is to write them. That's where the magic happens. When the words spit and drip onto the page, when the language turns lovely, when ideas and images touch paper or pixels, this is where the action is.

Yes, we all want to be published, be acknowledged, get famous, get rich. It's good stuff, and it helps drive us to continue on what is often a difficult and lonely path. But at the end of the day, worldly success is largely about ego.

Ego, in my super simplified definition, is all about our limited sense of self. If you don't win the award or get the standing ovation or make the big bucks, your ego is delighted to remind you that you suck and that you and your endeavors are worthless.

As you may have guessed, the ego is the twisted little sister of the Ic.

If your intention turns primarily towards money, recognition or any other kind of ego boost, danger lurks. It won't be long before you resent what you once loved because the outcome didn't match your expectation. Not cool. That's a lose/lose.

If you point your intention to what you love, and remember that the outcome you desire is just the frosting, your passion stays true.

If you genuinely allow yourself to play, to flow and curve and become light and fun, you will always win on some level. Whatever you choose to do will have value simply because you are doing it.

Didja hear that?

If you're playful in what you do, you will always succeed on some level because the play itself has value, regardless of the outcome.

Cool, right?

I spent much of my young adulthood frantically pursuing my dream of being a rockstar. I banged my head against wall after wall attempting to realize my vision. Finally, after years in the trenches, I landed not one, but three international record deals for my project Electron Love Theory. The album was electronic versions of U2 songs with female singers. Fan. F*ing. Tastic!

I'll spare you the gory details of the (temporary) murder of my heart and just say this. All three deals turned out to be absolutely devastating. Everything I worked for, dreamed of and sweated over transformed into a horrific experience worse than anything I could have ever imagined.

My music was beyond dissed. My dreams were consciously and maliciously pissed on. And I ended up paying my attorney big bucks to get into (and out of!) all of these deals. It was an epic, galactic level sh*t storm.

When the dust finally cleared I took some time to think about the whole thing. I realized that although the outcome of my efforts was nowhere near what I intended, I still loved the music I made. I was still thrilled to crank it up and listen to what I'd created. It was still the best recordings I had ever produced. Maybe that was enough.*

* Electron Love Theory's U2 ReVision is now an independent release streaming out all around the world. Over a million spins on Pandora alone. Ha!

Check this out.

Living an NFA life doesn't always need to be goal oriented.

At its core **NFA** is not actually about completing your goals, although that's great if you do. **Not F*ing Around** is a much bigger philosophy.

The play itself is the win. Writing the poem is the win. Recording the cover of your favorite U2 song is the win. Designing the perfect summer dress is the win.

NFA is really about playfully interacting with the world, and continuing to play with it, rather than achieving, winning or succeeding.

This is such an enormous (and counter-intuitive) piece. But the element of play, and non-attachment to the outcome, not only lubricates your connection to your heart and creativity, it actually increases your likelihood of achieving your goal. But it only works if the play and non-attachment are genuine and authentic.

Here's the even cooler part.

If it is genuine and authentic, it doesn't really matter if you achieve your goal or not because you truly love the process.

Crush on the process. Then step back and watch goodness unfold as the Universe connects you with all kinds of opportunities, fun and amazingness that you might not have anticipated.

Let go of your version of the ideal outcome.

When you create with Truth the Universe knows it and will give you back something valuable.

Remember what Mick taught us?

Something about not always getting what you want. But you kinda sorta somehow get what you need.

F*
Around

For all of the yak-yak on these pages, you'd think that I'm prescribing that every minute of every day ought to be **NFA**. Not so! While it is true that the more you crank up the **NFA**, the more pleasure, joy and connection will come to you, it's equally true that we all need some FA time.

FA is not a negative thing. It's not lazy or boring. It's necessary. And it's good for you.

As you may suspect, there's balance in the Universe. And too much **NFA** can knock you out of whack. So remember to chill out.

Breathe, rest, screw around. Get off topic. Wander. Defocus. Have a drink. Sleep in. Watch Simpsons reruns.

While it may appear to be a waste of time, it's not. It helps you refuel so that when you switch back to **NFA** mode the engine is warmed up and ready to go.

The bottom line.

Although it may not seem like it at times, every moment that you're alive on this planet is a big deal. It's also an opportunity. An opportunity to learn, to grow, to do stuff. It's an opportunity to love and expand and experience life.

You can choose random distractions, internet worm holes, crap jobs, dissonance, pessimism and heaviness. **Or you can choose Love**. And make your choices based on Love. If you do, your world opens up, your heart sings.

You may shout praises of the **NFA** lifestyle on the street or be busy perfecting your mind-blowing red velvet cake recipe, folding paper dragons or plotting out your new sci-fi trilogy. You may meet fascinating new friends, find yourself at the crossroads of small miracles and/or unforeseen opportunities. You might surface in a happy space that didn't exist in your world before.

Not F*ing Around is a philosophy, a way of being in and with the experience of life. It's rocket fuel to get the motor running and spark up the high powered creativity, imagination and magic that are just waiting to bust out in your life.

Do yourself a favor—

- Discover what you love. (And why.)
- Declare your dream.
- Time travel with your future self.
- Start before you're ready.
- Fail fast.
- Say "Yes, and_____."
- Be the shining star you are.
- Play it unsafe.
- F* the Ic.
- Crush on the process.
- F* around.

I sincerely and deeply hope this book charges you up in a big way. I hope you turn onto your dreams and make them happen. I hope your light burns bright and you inspire your communities and your Universe with goodness, value and amazing possibilities.

The more people who align their lives with love, passion and action, the better the world becomes for everyone.

The hours of this Earth trip are tick-tocking away every single minute of every single day for every single one of us.

Make them count.

N
F
A

Thanks for reading!

Want more **NFA**? Hell yeah you do.

Get the **newsletter**– blog posts, videos, interviews with NFA creatives, worksheets and other coolness.

Click on >>> JeffLeisawitz.com

Dig this book? F* right!
Go ahead... **send it to your pals**. Or better yet, ask them to download it from my site (along with lots of other goodies).

I want to hear from you. **Email me!**
Jeff@JeffLeisawitz.com

Thank you.

Thank you **magic** and **mystery**. **Creativity** and **darkness**.

Thank you technology and **intuition**, music and movies.

Thank you **language** and **rhythm**, **beauty**, **grace** and **chaos**.

Thank you camera, guitar, software.

Thank you **people**. Megan for the toons. Steve for believing. Moses for saving my ass (again). Eryn for opening my heart into new worlds of love and service.

Thank you **friends, collaborators, fans, followers, clients** and **students** for supporting the dream—step by step by step.

Thank you **fam** for always being there.

Thank you for reading. And for having the courage to step it up and get **NFA**.

Jeff Leisawitz burns with a mission— to inspire writers, artists, filmmakers, musicians and every other creative human to amp up their creativity, heal their hearts and shine in the world.

Jeff is an award-winning musician/ producer, a college instructor, speaker, photographer, critically acclaimed author and internationally distributed filmmaker who has devoted his life to empowering and inspiring creativity.

Not F*ing Around— The No Bullsh*t Guide for Getting Your Creative Dreams Off the Ground is Jeff's first book.

CPSIA information can be obtained
at www.ICGtesting.com
Printed in the USA
FSHW04n1755050418
46303FS